"Mirrors can
lucky for you 1
laugh either!"

"If had a dollar for every
smart thing you say.
I'll be poor."

"I'm not saying I hate you,
what I'm saying is that you are
literally the Monday of my life."

"I'm sorry I hurt your feelings when I called you stupid. I really thought you already knew."

"Unless your name is Google stop acting like you know everything."

"Just because I don't care doesn't mean I don't understand."

"Sarcasm is the secret language that everyone uses when they want to say something mean to your face."

"Always remember that you're unique. Just like everyone else."

"Accept that some days you are the pigeon, and some days you are the statue."

"I never forget a face,
but in your case,
I'll be glad to
make an exception."

"Everyone has the right to be
stupid, but you are abusing the
privilege!"

"People say that laughter
is the best medicine... your face
must be curing the world."

Life is good you should get one!

THOU
shalt
not
TRY ME

"My imaginary friend says that you need a therapist."

"Well, at least your mom thinks you're pretty."

"F*** you & your standards!"

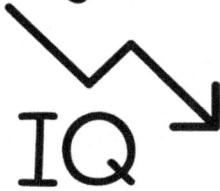

IQ

"Stupidity is not a crime,
so you're free to go."

"Never miss a good chance
to shut up."

"I feel so miserable without you, it's almost like having you here."

"If you wrote down every single thought you ever had you would get an award for the shortest story ever."

"I'll try being nicer if you try being smarter."

"If it looks like I give a damn,
please tell me.
I don't want to give off
the wrong impression."

"If ignorance is bliss.
You must be the happiest person
on this planet."

"Shut the F*** up and stop
complaining."

"Don't take life so seriously,
it isn't permanent."

"Cancel my subscription because
I don't need your issues."

"I'm sorry while you were talking
I was trying to figure where
the hell you got the idea
I cared."

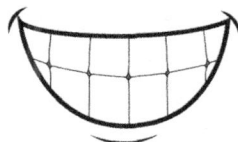

"No, you don't have to repeat yourself. I was ignoring you the first time." ☺

"I don't have the energy to pretend to like you today." ☺

"I would like to apologize to anyone I have not offended yet. Please be patient. I will get to you shortly."

"If you're waiting for me to give a shit, you better pack a lunch. It's going to be while."

"You'd be in good shape... if you ran as much as your mouth."

"Ugliness can be fixed, stupidity is forever."

"My silence doesn't mean I agree with you. It's just that your level of ignorance has rendered me speechless."

"You're everything I want in someone I don't want anymore."

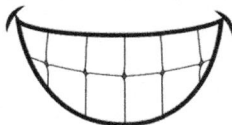

"Sometimes I meet people and feel bad for their dog."

"You play the victim.
I'll play the disinterested
bystander."

"I'll try being nicer,
if you try being smarter."

"Tact is for people who aren't
witty enough to use sarcasm."

"People think I go out of my way to piss them off. Trust me, it's not out of my way at all."

"No, no, no. I'm not insulting you. I'm just describing you."

"Your fervent, misguided sense of entitlement is stunning."

"I'm not listening, but keep talking. I enjoy the way your voice makes my ears bleed."

"That is the ugliest top I've ever seen, yet it compliments your face perfectly."

"If you're waiting for me to give a shit, you better pack a lunch. It's going to be while."

"I'd agree with you but then we'd both be wrong."

"Common sense is like deodorant. The people who need it most never use it."

"There's someone for everyone that person for you is a psychiatrist."

"Not a single one of my multiple personalities like you."

"I'll always cherish the original misconception I had of you."

"I'm sorry, I don't take orders. I barely take suggestions."

"Don't confuse a smile with someone baring teeth."

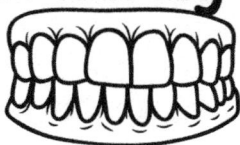

"We all know someone who speaks fluent crap."

"They say ignorance is bliss but I find yours rather disturbing."

"You can be whatever you want;
however, in your case
you should probably aim low."

"I lost your number.
I lost it when I hit 'delete.'"

"I wish more people were
fluent in silence."

"I found your nose.
It was in my business."

"Life is full of disappointments
and I just added you to the list."

When my friend's dog died, I tried
to cheer him up by getting him an
identical one. But he screamed at
me asking what he was supposed
to do with two dead dogs!

You are what you eat.
So, you should really give up the nuts.

Before I judge someone,
I walk a mile in their shoes.
So when I do judge them,
I am a mile away and I also
have their shoes.

A recent study has found that
the women who carry a bit of
extra weight live longer compared
to the men who mention it.

Did something awful happen to you or are naturally this dreadful of a person?

If you need more space, there is NASA.

How do you know that light travels faster than sound? A lot of people seem bright until they talk.

"If I promise to miss you, will you go away?"

"A pessimist's blood type is always b-negative."

"Never test the depth of the water with both feet."

Why should you stop trying if you don't succeed at first?
Because you're probably plain dumb.

How to be a nice boss?
You tell your employees,
"Don't consider me as your boss.
But think of me as a friend who has the power to fire you."

"It's okay if you don't like me. Not everyone has good taste."

"I don't believe in plastic surgery,
But in your case, Go ahead."

"You look good when your eyes
are closed, but you look the best
when my eyes closed."

"If you find me offensive.
Then I suggest you
quit finding me."

"I'm sorry while you were talking
I was trying to figure
where the hell you got the idea
I cared."

"I never forget a face, but in your
case, I'll be glad to make an
exception."

"My neighbor's diary says
that I have boundary issues."

"The stuff you heard about me is a lie. I'm way worse."

"Sometimes I wish I were a nicer person, but then I laugh and continue my day."

"Fun fact: Alcohol increases the size of the 'send' button by 89%."

"I don't keep secrets, I just keep people out of my business."

"Sorry for being late. I got caught up enjoying my last few minutes of you not being here."

"Sure I'll help you out... the same way you came in."

"My neighbors listen to good music whether they like it or not." 🙂

"I was asked what I look for in a relationship. Apparently 'a way out' wasn't the right answer."

"My boss said I intimidate my co-workers. I stared at him until he apologized." 🙂

"Instead of 'have a nice day,' I think I'll start saying, 'have the day you deserve.' You know, let karma sort things out."

"Nice perfume. Must you marinate in it?"

"Apparently rock bottom has a basement."

"Someday, you'll go far.
I hope you stay there."

"You couldn't handle me even
if I came with instructions."

"It's ok if you disagree with me.
I can't force you to be right."

Never tell your problems
to anyone...
20% don't care and the other
80% are glad you have them...

I'm not your type.
I'm not inflatable.

"I'm not always rude and sarcastic.
Sometimes I'm asleep."

"If someone asks, 'Are you crazy?'
Simply reply, 'Yes.'
Boom. End of discussion."

I hope your day is as
pleasant as you are.

Life's like a bird. It's pretty cute
until it shits on your head.

Most people are shocked when they find out how bad I am as an electrician. :D

I don't have an attitude problem. You have a perception problem.

You have not been yourself lately. We have all noticed the improvement.

Oops, my bad. I could've sworn I was dealing with an adult.

Oh, you don't like being treated the way you treat me? That must suck.

You're a gray sprinkle on a rainbow cupcake.

If your brain was dynamite, there wouldn't be enough to blow your hat off.

It's impossible to underestimate you.

Wow, your maker really didn't waste time giving you a personality, huh?

I'll never forget the first time we met. But I'll keep trying.

You're cute. Like my dog. He also chases his tail for entertainment. LOL!

You are like a cloud. When you disappear, it's a beautiful day. HAHA

You have an entire life to be an idiot. Why not take today off?

OUCH

Your face is just fine, but we'll have to put a bag over that personality.

Don't worry, the first 40 years of childhood are always the hardest.

If you have a problem with me,
write the problem on
a piece of paper,
fold it, and shove it up your ass.

I thought of you today.
It reminded me to take out
the trash.

Did the mental hospital test too
many drugs on you today?

I forgot the world
revolves around you.
My apologies, how silly of me.

When you look in the mirror,
say hi to the clown you see in
there for me, would you?

Your secrets are always
safe with me. I never even listen
when you tell me them.

Somewhere out there is a tree tirelessly producing oxygen for you. You owe it an apology.

Don't worry about me. Worry about your eyebrows.

You just might be why the middle finger was invented in the first place.

You must have been
born on a highway.
That's where most
accidents happen.

Take my lowest priority
and put yourself beneath it.

Hey, you have something
on your chin.
No, the 3rd one down.

You're my favorite person...
besides every other person I've
ever met.

You are proof that evolution
can go in reverse.

I would prefer a battle of wits,
but you appear unarmed.

When I see your face, there's not a thing that I would change... except the direction I was walking in.

I would never date you. I'm lonely, not desperate.

I'd say you're 'dumb as a rock,' but at least a rock can hold a door open.

Somewhere, somehow, you are robbing a village of their idiot.

You are the reason why shampoo has instructions.

If you were the light at the end of the tunnel, I'd turn back around.

Were you born this stupid
or did you take lessons?

I don't know what your
problem is, but I'm guessing it's
hard to pronounce.

The people who tolerate you
on a daily basis are
the real heroes.

Jesus might love you, but everyone else definitely thinks you're an idiot.

You're about as useful as an ashtray on a motorcycle.

Aww, it's so cute when you try to talk about things you don't understand.

As an outsider,
what do you think of
the human race?

You're living proof it's possible
to live without a brain.

I'd be happy to hear from you if
you were actually important.

If I said anything to offend you it was purely intentional.

I have seen people like you. But I had to pay admission.

The last time I saw a face like yours, I fed it a banana.

You fear success, but you really have nothing to worry about.

If I wanted to hear from an asshole, I'd fart.

I'd give you a nasty look, but you've already got one.

Printed in Great Britain
by Amazon